Avatar

by Melaina Faranda
illustrated by Renée Nault

Contents

Predators

A sudden, sharp pain made him stop, but there was no time, not if he wanted to get away from them with only an achingly black bruise. He should never have tried to defend Lan. Kevin was used to being picked on, but it had made his blood boil to see them taunting her. When she'd finally put her book down, he had seen tears glistening in her dark, crescent-moon eyes.

Kevin was used to being picked on

Close Reading

What mood does the author create in the opening scene? List and explain specific language or details to support your answer.

The stone that had hit his neck now winked evilly from where it had landed in the parched grass. Kevin stared at the stone's razor edge. What would have happened if it had hit his head?

Shuddering, he put his hand to the back of his neck and felt the roughness of grazed skin.

circling the
edge of the
vacant lot like
hungry wolves

4

They'd taken his cap, which Jamie had subsequently rubbed into dog droppings in the vacant lot. Then the three boys had chased after him, waving the cap and yelling: "Come back here and put your hat on, dork boy!"

Kevin jolted into action. Stumbling onward, he rounded the corner and hurtled down the street of identical brick houses where he lived. Behind him, his tormentors were circling the edge of the vacant lot like hungry wolves, and he could still hear them calling.

Kevin passed Mrs. Delaney's garden, with its gnomes and ceramic snails and plastic, pink flamingos, and then he ran on to Mrs. Azzapardi's house. The dusty smell of wet cement filled Kevin's nostrils. Mrs. Azzapardi was out front, hosing the concrete beneath the grape trellis. She pointed a plump arm in his direction, and a jet of icy water sprayed all over him.

"Why are you always running around like this when it's so terribly hot?" she shouted after him.

Kevin shook his head and, like a dog, furiously flicked off the water. He wasn't hot anymore, but now his schoolbooks would be soaked. He'd be in trouble again at school; although at least this time, it was only tap water. A week ago, his bag had been dunked in a toilet.

First Reading

How does Kevin escape from the bullies?

The Game

His house was empty, as he'd known it would be. Luckily, Jamie and his cronies didn't. Kevin tugged out the key that he kept on a length of string around his neck, since he couldn't risk leaving it in his backpack or pocket, where anything could happen to it. His house was fast becoming the only place he was safe, but he also knew that it was only a matter of time before they attacked him here as well.

A sickly wave of perfume and stale cigarettes enveloped him the moment he opened the door. She'd been home that morning.

Kevin peered through the open door of his mother's bedroom. On her dressing table, one of her many lipstick tubes had been carelessly left open, its scarlet color gleaming wetly in the light that filtered through the sheet tacked over the window. He replaced the lipstick cap and continued to the kitchen.

Inside the fridge were rows of chocolate bars, half a carton of milk, and the leftovers from last night's takeout. Kevin grabbed a chocolate bar and went to his room.

Neon lights glowed in the darkness, welcoming him. Kevin threw his bag down and switched on the computer. The gentle hum of its start-up instantly soothed him, while at the same time, a roar of adrenaline filled him as he typed in the title of the video game. A tall, heavily muscled figure with depthless eyes and a rock-like jaw grinned back at him. Himself. In the real world. His avatar.

"What is our mission today?" the avatar droned.

Kevin smiled and leaned back into his chair. He typed with two fingers: "We must fly over the wastelands to fight the evil Jamaster and rescue Princess Lana."

The avatar raised his sword and whistled for their war chariot. Kevin had painstakingly fashioned it from a mix of World War II fighter planes and the latest high-tech space shuttles.

He wished he could stay in this world forever

"It will be a pleasure," the avatar intoned.

"A pleasure," Kevin agreed. Already he felt taller, stronger, and more powerful. As he mentally hopped into the craft with his avatar, he wished he could stay in this world forever.

Close Reading

What two types of violence has the author explored so far in the book?

Sanctuary

Kevin's heart pounded. Jamie and the others snuck out of the school lunchroom and down the hall toward him. Kevin quickened his pace and slipped, just in time, through the sliding glass doors and into his sanctuary. Mr. O'Dowd looked up from a book catalog and gave a brief nod of recognition. Kevin had become a regular in the lunchtime huddle of library kids.

Jamie and the others barged in noisily behind him.

Mr. O'Dowd raised his gingery eyebrows and tapped impatiently on the counter. "Are you boys looking for anything in particular?"

Jamie darted Kevin a narrow-eyed promise of later pain. "Come on," he ordered his two friends. "Let's get out of nerd central."

Kevin drifted through the long, quiet rows of books: history, science, biology, mythology, and technology. He wondered if he should have simply let Jamie thump him rather than carry this sickening dread around with him. Yesterday afternoon and evening, he had taken great satisfaction in letting the avatar take revenge on Jamaster. Kevin had been thrilled by the fury of the avatar's attack. Then, rescuing Princess Lana, it had been impossible to stop his avatar from kissing her . . .

Heat rose in Kevin's cheeks at the memory of how she had clung to him, her long silk dress swirling around their feet, her beautiful black hair billowing out into the rosy cyber sunset.

First Reading

Why does the library become Kevin's sanctuary?

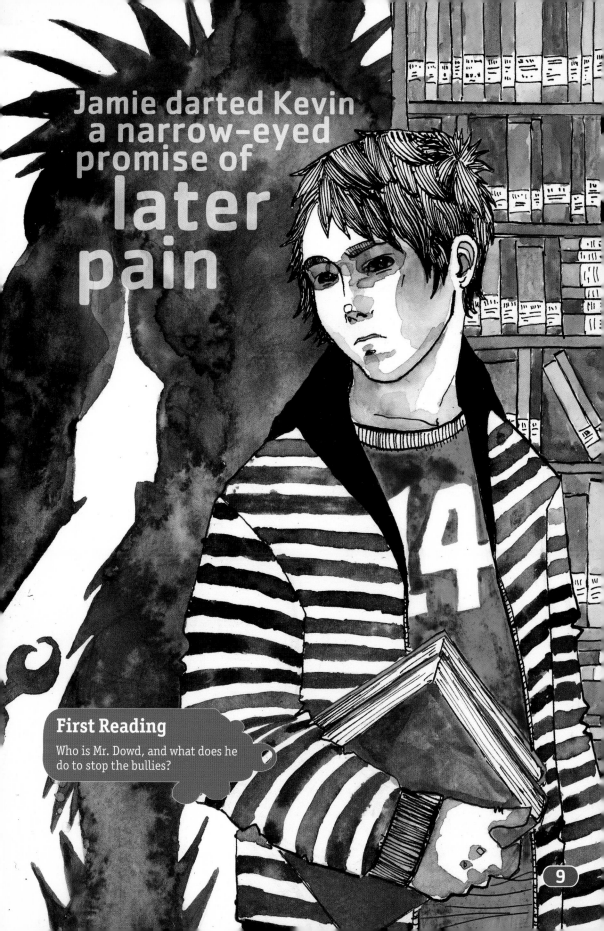

Jamie darted Kevin a narrow-eyed promise of **later pain**

First Reading

Who is Mr. Dowd, and what does he do to stop the bullies?

9

Secret Names

"Kevin?"

The voice jolted him out of his pleasant daydream. Lan sat curled on the seat next to him with a brick-sized dictionary.

He blushed. "Oh . . . er, hi!"

Ever since Lan had first arrived at school, he had longed to talk to her. In history class, he sat at the desk directly behind hers. While Ms. Janaki droned on, he stared at Lan's shiny black hair and her neat, delicate earlobes with their tiny dragon earrings.

Now Kevin wished again that he could be more like his avatar. He wanted to impress her. Avatar would be smooth and in control and know what to say, but this was the school library, and Kevin was just some uncool kid who had no idea how to make her like him.

"Thank you for defending me yesterday," Lan said quietly.

At the memory of her silent tears, Kevin's fists bunched at his sides. He could feel the rough edges of his chewed fingernails digging into his palms. "Don't listen to them. They're pigs."

Lan burst into laughter.

"What's so funny?" Kevin asked, hoping she wasn't laughing at him.

Lan's dark eyes became solemn. "I am sorry, but in my country there are many pigs in the street. They have such little eyes and hairy skin. Like Jamie."

Kevin smiled. "What is your country like?" he asked. He had been intrigued from the moment Ms. Janaki had clucked around Lan and introduced her to the class as a "special new student all the way from Vietnam."

"Noisy," Lan said. "There are people everywhere, cooking and selling things. Animals wander around the streets."

"Pigs?" Kevin asked with a grin.

Lan nodded. "And dogs and ducks. And there are dragons," she added dreamily. "Beautiful dragons with precious stones under their tongues. Dragons that can breathe fire or water."

First Reading

Why does Kevin want to be more like his avatar?

"Dragons?" Kevin repeated. He hoped she wasn't trying to make a fool of him.

"Ones made of red silk and gold paper," Lan said. "We can only have power over them if we know their secret names."

Kevin thought about the silent suburban streets surrounding his school, places without dragons or ducks or people. "Why did you come here?"

The sparkle in Lan's eyes faded, and her dark gaze was haunted. "My parents say it wasn't safe there. We left two years ago, after my brother stepped on a land mine."

First Reading

Why did Lan's family leave Vietnam?

Siren Call

Without thinking, Kevin reached out to pat her shoulder. He couldn't imagine what she must have been feeling, since he himself had never experienced such a tragedy.

"Going to kiss her, dork boy?"

Kevin swivelled around to find Jamie leering at them from between two tall metal bookshelves.

he was going to a place where he could be strong

Mr. O'Dowd was not behind the counter to save them. There was only a supervising student teacher banging the photocopier lid up and down.

"Leave us alone," Kevin muttered.

"Yeah? Who's going to make me?" Lunging like a bird of prey, Jamie belted him in the gut, and Kevin doubled over, groaning. "Like punching a couch cushion," he said disgustedly. "You're as weak as my baby brother."

"Leave him alone!" Lan cried. "You go away." She rushed to Kevin and put her arm around him. "Miss! Miss!" she shouted.

At the far end of the library, the student teacher looked up, saw Jamie, sighed, and then went back to her photocopying.

"That's quite enough, young man." Mr. O'Dowd appeared at last. He looked at Jamie as if he were something to be wiped off his shoe. "Unless you intend to borrow a book about social etiquette, get out. Now."

Jamie rolled his eyes. "Later," he mouthed to Kevin before slouching back out of the library.

"Are you OK?" Lan asked worriedly.

Kevin shrugged, humiliated by the way he had crumpled in front of her. He gave a short laugh. "Sure. I have to go." There was no way he was hanging around like sucker bait until school was out.

He snuck out through the back of the school, past the scabby pine trees and through the shopping center parking lot. More than ever, Kevin heard the silent siren call of the avatar. He was going to a place where he could be strong. Powerful. Invincible.

Close Reading

What mythological creature does the chapter's title refer to? How does understanding the tale of the siren enhance your reading of the text?

Jamaster

Avatar left the warship parked in the vast hangars of his space palace. Instead, he rode a scarlet and gold dragon. It had the head of a camel, bulbous and smoldering eyes, the twisting body of a snake, and a tiger's claws. They winged their way swiftly to Jamaster's realm. The villain would have to be punished.

Flying over magestically purple rivers and spiky mountains that spewed golden fire, they reached the deadened black earth of Jamaster's kingdom. It was an evil place, spewing sulphurous yellow-green smoke. Winged hybrid cyber creatures spat and shot target-seeking barbs into intruders.

Effortlessly, Avatar repelled these creatures with their multiple eyes and strange, spiked heads. He blighted them with his sword. The dragon breathed ice to make the creatures freeze, so that they dropped like grotesque statues onto the festering land below.

Jamaster's castle was a circle of shining black metal. Avatar laughed at the evil lord's minions with their piggy snouts and beady red eyes. He slashed at them with his sword. "Here, piggy, piggy!"

Avatar waded through the carnage. Jamaster was hiding in the inner chamber, clutching Princess Lana with one hand. With the other, Jamaster pressed a razor-fine lightblade to her throat. "Drop your weapon. Any closer and . . . "

Jamaster smiled nastily and looked pointedly at the lightblade. Lana's eyes widened with terror.

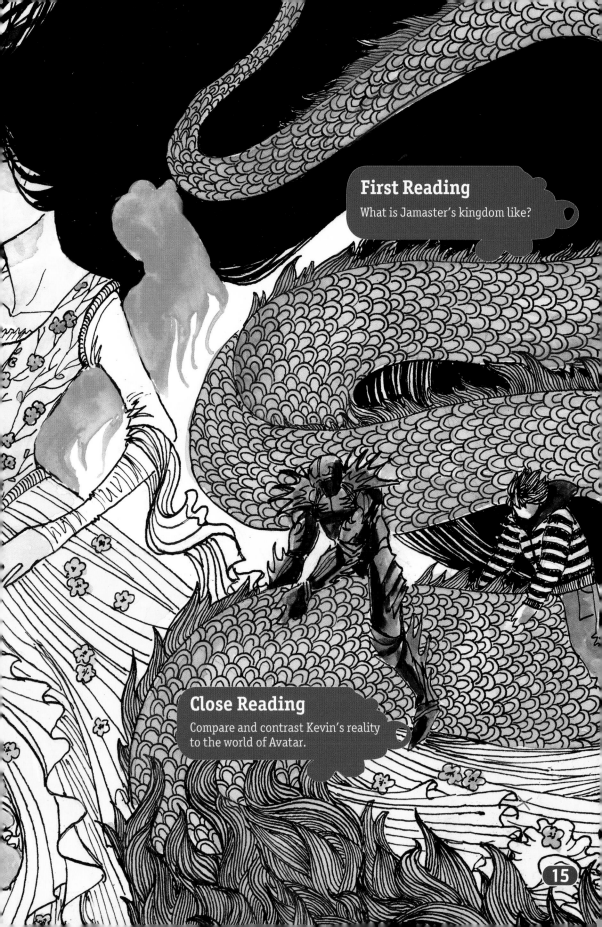

First Reading

What is Jamaster's kingdom like?

Close Reading

Compare and contrast Kevin's reality to the world of Avatar.

Dragon Tears

Avatar reluctantly lowered his sword.

Jamaster laughed. "Weak," he sneered. "Weak as . . . "

The chamber erupted. Shards flew around the room as a scarlet and gold dragon burst in, flexing its sabre-like claws.

The princess leapt away from where Jamaster had fallen to the ground, then she raced to the dragon. The dragon and the girl looked at each other intently, and she whispered its secret name.

Instantly, the dragon's tongue unfurled like a long red ribbon. Princess Lana reached in and withdrew a sparkling diamond the size of a small duck's egg or a dragon's tear.

Avatar put his powerful arms around her slender waist. She craned her face up to meet his, and . . .

"Kevvy, sweetie, is that you?"

What was his mother doing home? Kevin cursed and turned off the monitor just as his door flew open.

His mother wore a faded sweatshirt and tracksuit pants instead of her usual skirt and heels. Her lips looked weirdly pale, and her mascara had run, making her sad brown eyes like those of a frightened animal.

Kevin guessed that she'd broken up with the latest guy even before his mother said dully, "Dave ended it. He didn't think I was the one."

He moved forward and awkwardly hugged her.

"Why doesn't it ever work out?" she moaned. "What's wrong with me? All I ever wanted was to find my Prince Charming, my soul mate . . . "

Kevin closed his eyes, dreading what always came next.

"Dave's just like your father," she hissed. "No good. Your father left me as soon as you came along."

He couldn't bear it. He had to get away. "Mom, I'll go get some takeout. Pizza?" He knew she'd only pick off the pepperoni, and he'd get to eat the whole pizza by himself.

"I'm sick of pizza. Get me something different."

Kevin fled into the night.

Dave hadn't been the one. Same with Frank and Giovanni and Paul and all the others with their fast, flashy cars. When would she learn to live in the real world?

First Reading

How does Princess Lana retrieve the diamond from the dragon?

Strange Song

White streetlights glared down on Mrs. Delaney's plastic flamingos, and sprinklers ticked over Mrs. Azzapardi's lawn. Warm smells of cooking wafted out onto the road, which made Kevin even hungrier as he trudged several blocks over to a strip of takeout restaurants he rarely visited.

The enticing aroma of hamburgers and French fries lured him into the first restaurant he came to, but he ducked instantly out of sight. Jamie and his friends were playing the old-style pinball machine.

A block farther up was a restaurant with red and gold plastic fans arranged across a ledge. An octagonal mirror flashed above the entrance. There was a rush of spicy air as the door opened.

"Kevin!"

"Oh . . . hi!"

Lan looked older than she did at school. She wore her hair up and a narrow red satin dress that buttoned at the side. She smiled. "Come and meet my family."

First Reading

Why does Lan's grandmother beam at Kevin?

Kevin allowed himself to be led through a scattering of tables set with chopsticks and paper napkins and into the kitchen. Inside, dark-haired people of assorted ages chopped vegetables and stirred steaming pots. The way they called to each other sounded like a strange song, but it was very beautiful.

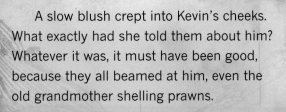

Lan pulled him deeper into the kitchen and spoke to her family in the same singsong way.

Then she said in English, "This is my friend from school. Kevin. The one I told you about."

A slow blush crept into Kevin's cheeks. What exactly had she told them about him? Whatever it was, it must have been good, because they all beamed at him, even the old grandmother shelling prawns.

"They like you," Lan said, pleased. "My grandmother says you must eat. What would you like?"

This wasn't going to be a place that sold burgers. He had never eaten Vietnamese food before.

Seeing his confusion, Lan's eyes grew mischievous. "What about pork rolls?"

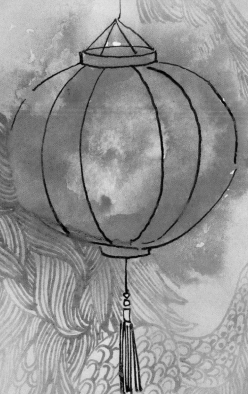

Close Reading

What verbs does the author use to make Kevin's journey to the restaurant even more vivid?

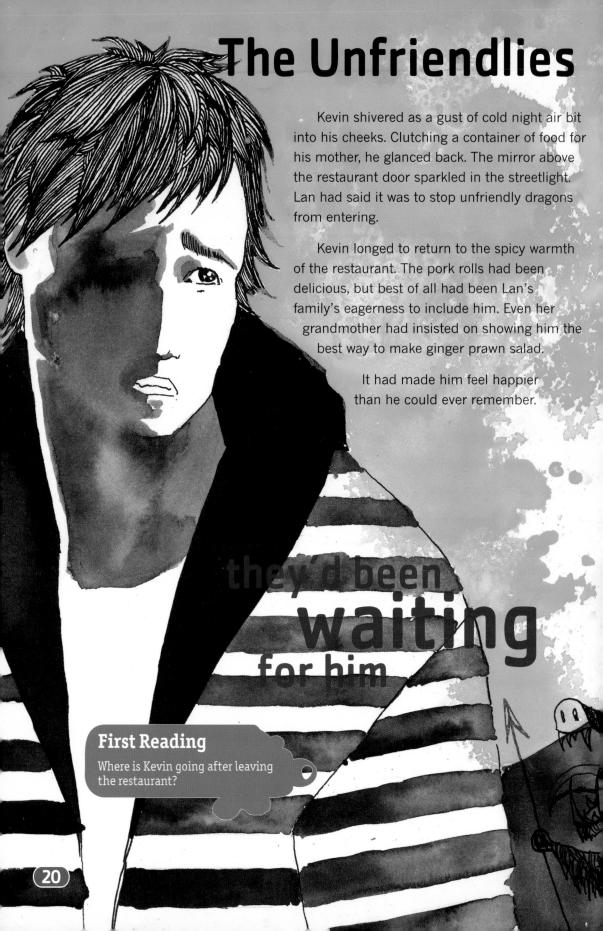

The Unfriendlies

Kevin shivered as a gust of cold night air bit into his cheeks. Clutching a container of food for his mother, he glanced back. The mirror above the restaurant door sparkled in the streetlight. Lan had said it was to stop unfriendly dragons from entering.

Kevin longed to return to the spicy warmth of the restaurant. The pork rolls had been delicious, but best of all had been Lan's family's eagerness to include him. Even her grandmother had insisted on showing him the best way to make ginger prawn salad.

It had made him feel happier than he could ever remember.

they'd been **waiting** for him

First Reading

Where is Kevin going after leaving the restaurant?

20

A low hiss made him spin around. Beyond the perimeter of the streetlight were three bunched-up shadows. They'd been waiting for him.

Kevin tried to run, but happiness and a full stomach had made him slow. They grabbed him and pulled him into the shadows, against a prickly hedge.

"Been with your girlfriend?" Jamie taunted.

He pulled his eyes into slits with his fingers, then pushed Kevin straight into the arms of one of his thugs.

"Don't you say a word about her!" Kevin shouted. "You leave Lan out of this. If you want to pick on someone, pick on me."

"My pleasure," Jamie said.

Close Reading

Summarize what you know about the characters, using evidence from the text and any inferences you have made.

they'll never
hurt you or me again

First Reading

What gives Kevin the strength to
fight back?

Avatar's Revenge

Jamie jabbed a fist into Kevin's ribs, and he grunted with pain. With the next blow, he dropped the food for his mother. There was a wet, garlicky slap of rice noodles and prawns.

When he saw Lan's grandmother's food slicked over the pavement, Kevin's pain gave way to fury. Like a volcano, it forced its way up and erupted. He felt as if his body was changing. Pure, raw energy stiffened the loose flesh on his arms and legs and tightened his gut. Avatar. He was all-powerful, invincible.

Jamie backed away, his piggy eyes round with fear.

Kevin reached forward. He had no need of a sword. Instead, he grabbed Jamie's shoulders and shook him effortlessly until his head went floppy. He reached next for Jamie's cowering companions. As he tripped one with his foot, he heard a satisfying crunch. The other one didn't wait around.

"Kevin!" Lan called from the entrance of the restaurant. She raced over, followed by her family. When Lan saw Jamie's prone body and the other boy writhing in pain, she gave a small scream. "What happened?"

Another surge of power burned through him. He was no longer weak, bumbling Kevin. He was Avatar, and he wanted to grab the girl and crush her close to him. He had conquered; he was the victor.

Lan backed away. It was as if she didn't recognize him. Her family clustered around, moaning with distress. The gold dragons in Lan's ears seemed mottled and dull in the streetlight.

"I won," Kevin said. "Can't you see? I won. They'll never hurt you or me again."

"Go," Lan said simply, her eyes tired and sad. "Go."

Kevin strode through the streets as if he owned them. There was nothing and no one to be afraid of now. He kicked over Mrs. Delaney's stupid pink flamingos and pulled a bunch of grapes from Mrs. Azzapardi's trellis. He tossed the grapes into his mouth, one by one.

When he got home, Kevin saw that his mother had fallen asleep in front of the television. Usually, he would have helped her into bed or laid a blanket over her. Now, he felt pitiless. She was such a victim. Why didn't she just seize hold of the things she wanted and destroy the things she didn't?

Teacher from a Higher Realm

She avoided him. They all avoided him.

Lan didn't look up from her dictionary when he spoke to her.

Jamie, a supportive neck brace of foam around his neck, kept a wary distance.

His mother, drifting like a pale ghost through the house, was afraid to address him in case he snapped at her again to go and get a life.

Kevin felt miserable.

First Reading

Why does Lan disapprove of what Kevin did?

He was finally powerful and strong, the way he had always wished to be, and people feared him. The only person who grinned to see him was Avatar.

Together, they raged around the cyber world on the back of the dragon. Only something was wrong with the pixel coloring. The scarlet and gold had turned grey. Kevin knew that if he were to reach inside the dragon's mouth, there would be no jewel gleaming beneath its tongue.

Jamaster's realm had been destroyed, and all other missions seemed hollow. Princess Lana seemed more and more like a doll, hollowly carrying out his commands.

Kevin felt cheated. Lan was supposed to be impressed by his transformation. She was supposed to fall in love with him.

He found her in the school library and tried one last time. "Why won't you speak to me?"

Lan looked up over her dictionary and gazed at him searchingly. "You aren't who I thought you were."

"But what do you mean?" Kevin asked in frustration.

"I thought you were kind, and I liked that." She shuddered. "But then you changed. What you did to Jamie. You scared me. My family, too."

Unable to look her in the eye, Kevin idly flicked through the dictionary: avarice, avascular, avast . . .

"But I stopped them from picking on us."

Lan nodded grimly. "My family believes there should always be other ways than violence."

Although she did not say it, Kevin remembered Lan's earlier words: *My brother stepped on a land mine.*

He looked at her intently. "What if I change back to who I was? What if I show you who I really am?"

Lan smiled. "I'd like that a lot."

Close Reading

How does the line "Kevin felt cheated" relate to the book's theme of violence?

av·a·tar
1. Manifestat
superhuman
2. A teacher

what if I show you who I really am

Victory

This time, the start-up hum of the computer filled Kevin with dread. He tasted metallic fear in his mouth as he typed in the title of the game.

Avatar appeared with his sword, grinning.

"I'm sorry," Kevin whispered, "but I need to get the girl."

Avatar mounted the dragon, its scales gleaming scarlet and gold once more. "Mission?" he asked in his mechanical tone.

Kevin sighed. "Anywhere," he typed.

First Reading

What does Kevin do with his video game?

Avatar waited, his expression blank. "Who are our enemies in Anywhere?"

"There are no more enemies."

"Where is Anywhere?" Avatar droned.

Kevin thought about Lan and her family and how, after this was done, he would go to the restaurant. He would help her grandmother shell prawns and laugh with her cousins. He would feel safe showing them all who he really was. Lan would learn that, deep down, he could be trusted. It might take weeks or months, but then one day, one special day, they would kiss beneath the sparkling mirror that kept unfriendly dragons out . . .

"Far, far away," Kevin typed. He watched Avatar leap upon the dragon and fly into a purple swirl of clouds.

Kevin pulled the heavy curtain away from his window. Golden afternoon light sifted through the dusty panes. Outside, Mrs. Azzapardi chatted with Mrs. Delaney while her yappy dog turned somersaults around them.

Smiling, Kevin clicked: PROGRAM UNINSTALL.

Close Reading

What is the author's overall message about violence?

Think About the Text

MAKING CONNECTIONS

Which of the following connections can you make to the characters, plot, setting, and themes of *Avatar*?

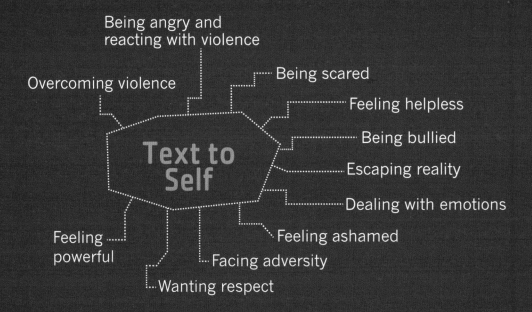

Being angry and reacting with violence

Being scared

Overcoming violence

Feeling helpless

Being bullied

Text to Self

Escaping reality

Dealing with emotions

Feeling powerful

Feeling ashamed

Facing adversity

Wanting respect

Text to Text/Media

Talk about texts/media you have read, listened to, or seen that have similar themes. Compare the treatment of theme and the differing author styles.

Text to World

Talk about situations in the world that connect to elements in the story.

Planning a Contemporary Fiction Story

Contemporary fiction incorporates many different genres, such as mystery, science fiction, adventure, narratives . . .

1 Think about what defines contemporary fiction

Contemporary fiction connects the reader with the complex situations and events of contemporary society. It incorporates themes and contexts that are seen as:

- a reflection of the past
- a mirror of the present
- an indicator of the future

2 Think about the plot

Decide on a plot that has an introduction, problems, and a solution. Write events in the order that they occur.

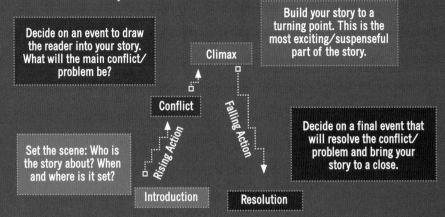

Decide on an event to draw the reader into your story. What will the main conflict/problem be?

Build your story to a turning point. This is the most exciting/suspenseful part of the story.

Climax

Conflict

Falling Action

Rising Action

Set the scene: Who is the story about? When and where is it set?

Decide on a final event that will resolve the conflict/problem and bring your story to a close.

Introduction

Resolution

Think about the sequence of events and how to present it using contemporary fiction devices, such as flashback and foreshadowing.

Flashback = showing part of the story line out of sequence

Foreshadowing = suggesting or indicating events before they happen

3 Think about the characters

Explore:

- How they think, feel and act

- What motivates their behavior

- Their inner feelings, using contemporary fiction approaches, such as stream of consciousness and product-of-society typecasting

Stream of consciousness = a description of the flow of thoughts and feelings through a character's mind as they arise

Product-of-society typecasting = giving the characters roles that are typical of the society they were born into

4 Decide on the setting

atmosphere/
mood

location

time

Note: Contemporary fiction provides a window into current lifestyles and living conditions, which are often shaped by multimedia influences.

Writing a Contemporary Fiction Story

Have you . . .

- made links to the society and events of your period?

- identified with recurrent contemporary themes?

- maintained a fast pace of action?

- grabbed the readers' attention and dragged them from the first page to the final page?

- been true to the context of your time frame?

- provided a window on the past or present or future?

- explored contemporary values and beliefs?

- developed characters that will stand up to in-depth analysis?

DON'T FORGET TO REVISIT YOUR WRITING.

DO YOU NEED TO CHANGE, ADD, OR DELETE ANYTHING TO IMPROVE YOUR STORY?